Commissioned by the Tanglewood Music Festival

COMPOSER'S NOTE

After composing *Syringa* in 1978 on a poem of John Ashbery, I have frequently returned to his poetry with the hope of finding texts that suggested musical settings. On learning that there might be a performance of some of my old choral works, and having heard how skillful modern choruses are, I decided to compose an a cappella vocal sextet on three Ashbery poems that attracted my attention, partly because of their sardonic humor (suggesting the title, *Mad Regales*) that implies a deeper undertone.

– Elliott Carter
August 1, 2007

Duration: 9 minutes

8 Haiku

Too low for nettles but it is exactly the way people think and feel
And it is a dream sailing in a dark unprotected cove
You lay aside your hair like a book that is too important to read now
In rags and crystals, sometimes with a shred of sense, an odd dignity
The dreams descend like cranes on gilded, forgetful wings
What trees, tools, why ponder socks on the premises
The wedding was enchanted everyone was glad to be in it
He is a monster like everyone else but what do you do if you're a monster

Meditations of a Parrot

Oh the rocks and the thimble
The oasis and the bed
Oh the jacket and the roses.
All sweetly stood up the sea to me
Like blue cornflakes in a white bowl.
The girl said, "Watch this."

I come from Spain, I said.
I was purchased at a fair.
She said, "None of us know."
"There was a house once
Of dazzling canopies
And halls like a keyboard.

"These the waves tore in pieces."
(His old wound –
And all day! Robin Hood! Robin
Hood!)

At North Farm

Someone somewhere is traveling furiously toward you,
At incredible speed, traveling day and night,
Through blizzards and desert heart, across torrents, through narrow passes.
But will he know where to find you,
Recognize you when he sees you,
Give you the thing he has for you?

Hardly anything grows here,
Yet the granaries are bursting with meal,
The sacks of meal piled to the rafters.
The streams run with sweetness, fattening fish;
Birds darken the sky. Is it enough
That the dish of milk is set out at night,
That we think of him sometimes,
Sometimes and always, with mixed feelings?

to Ellen Highstein

MAD REGALES
on poems of John Ashbery
for 6 Solo Voices

John Ashbery
** from: *37 HAIKU*

Elliott Carter
(2007)

I. 8 HAIKU **

8th Edition: 5 November 2008

ISMN 979-0-051-47850-7

Printed in U.S.A. 2008

2

CARTER: *Mad Regales*

CARTER: *Mad Regales*

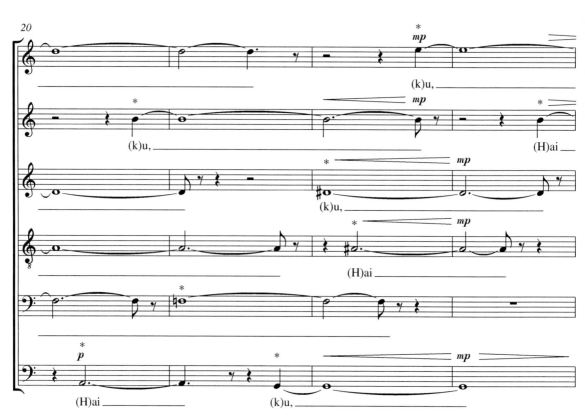

CARTER: *Mad Regales*

CARTER: *Mad Regales*

CARTER: *Mad Regales*

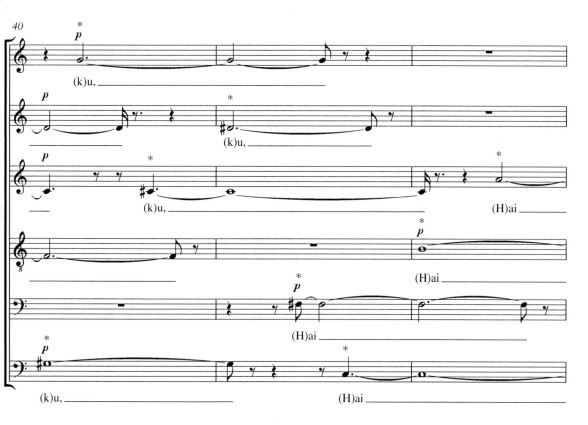

CARTER: *Mad Regales*

8

II. MEDITATIONS OF A PARROT

John Ashbery

Elliott Carter
(2007)

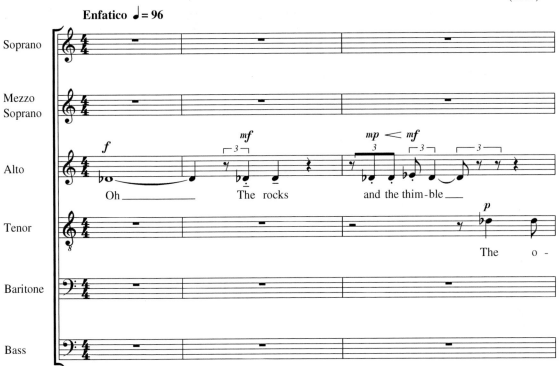

CARTER: *Mad Regales*

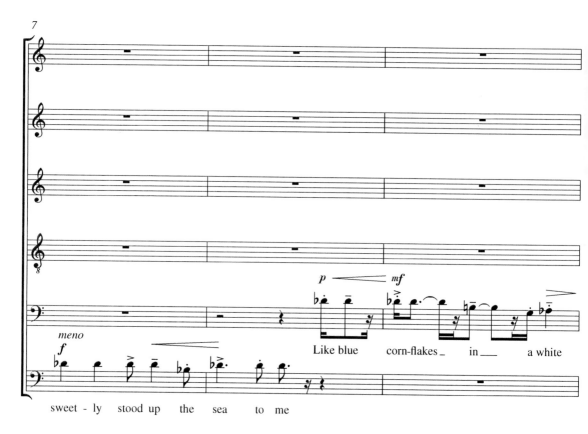

CARTER: *Mad Regales*

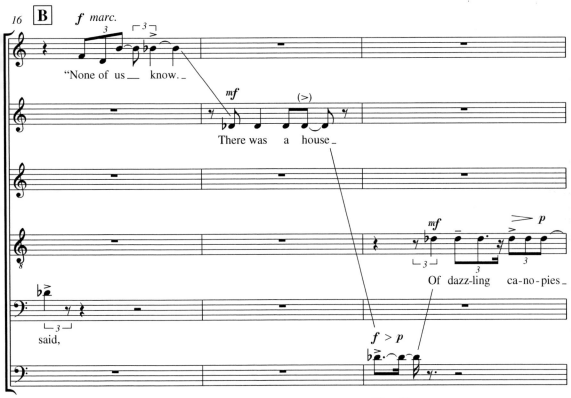

CARTER: *Mad Regales*

12

CARTER: *Mad Regales*

III. AT NORTH FARM

John Ashbery

Elliott Carter
(2007)

CARTER: *Mad Regales*

CARTER: *Mad Regales*

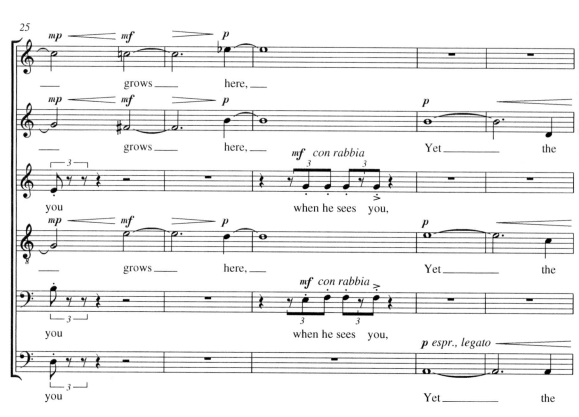

CARTER: *Mad Regales*

CARTER: *Mad Regales*

CARTER: *Mad Regales*

CARTER: *Mad Regales*

CARTER: *Mad Regales*